FREEDOM'S
PROMISE

BLACKS
IN PARIS

AFRICAN AMERICAN CULTURE IN EUROPE

BY DUCHESS HARRIS, JD, PHD
WITH ANITRA BUDD

Core Library

An Imprint of Abdo Publishing
abdobooks.com

Cover image: Josephine Baker performs at the Olympia
theater in Paris, France, in 1959.

abdocorelibrary.com

Printed in the United States of America, North Mankato, Minnesota
092018
012019

THIS BOOK CONTAINS
RECYCLED MATERIALS

Cover Photo: Keystone/Hulton Archive/Getty Images
Interior Photos: Keystone/Hulton Archive/Getty Images, 1; Lipnitzki/Roger Viollet/Getty Images,
5; Robert W. Kelley/The LIFE Picture Collection/Getty Images, 6–7; Frank W. Legg/U.S. National
Archives, 9; Everett Collection/Newscom, 12–13; Underwood Archives/UIG Universal Images
Group/Newscom, 15; Red Line Editorial, 18, 40; AP Images, 20–21, 26–27, 30–31, 33, 43; Mario
Torrisi/AP Images, 23; Christophe Ena/AP Images, 36–37

Editor: Maddie Spalding
Series Designer: Claire Vanden Branden

Library of Congress Control Number: 2018949704

Publisher's Cataloging-in-Publication Data

Names: Harris, Duchess, author. | Budd, Anitra, author.
Title: Blacks in Paris: African American culture in Europe / by Duchess Harris and
    Anitra Budd.
Other title: African American culture in Europe
Description: Minneapolis, Minnesota : Abdo Publishing, 2019 | Series: Freedom's
    promise | Includes online resources and index.
Identifiers: ISBN 9781532117671 (lib. bdg.) | ISBN 9781641856010 (pbk) | ISBN
    9781532170539 (ebook)
Subjects: LCSH: Black history--Juvenile literature. | Sociology--Europe--History--
    Juvenile literature. | Harlem Renaissance (Ciboure, France)--Juvenile
    literature.
Classification: DDC 944.3600--dc23

CONTENTS

A LETTER FROM DUCHESS

I asked my college students to name a city where many southern African Americans moved after World War I (1914–1918). Their responses included New York City; Chicago, Illinois; and Detroit, Michigan. These answers are correct. But one city that they did not mention was Paris, France.

After World War I broke out, more than 200,000 black soldiers came to France to fight for freedom and democracy. When they were in Paris, they were treated as human beings. Back in the United States, there were Ku Klux Klan members who might lynch them if they had on a uniform. Because of this, many African Americans stayed in Paris.

African American culture took off in France between World War I and World War II (1939–1945). The French discovered African-American music. Club owners fought to get black bands during the Jazz Age. Please join me on a journey to learn about blacks in Paris. This is a story about the promise of freedom in the City of Lights.

Duchess Harris

Louis Armstrong and many other jazz musicians performed in Paris during their careers.

CHAPTER ONE

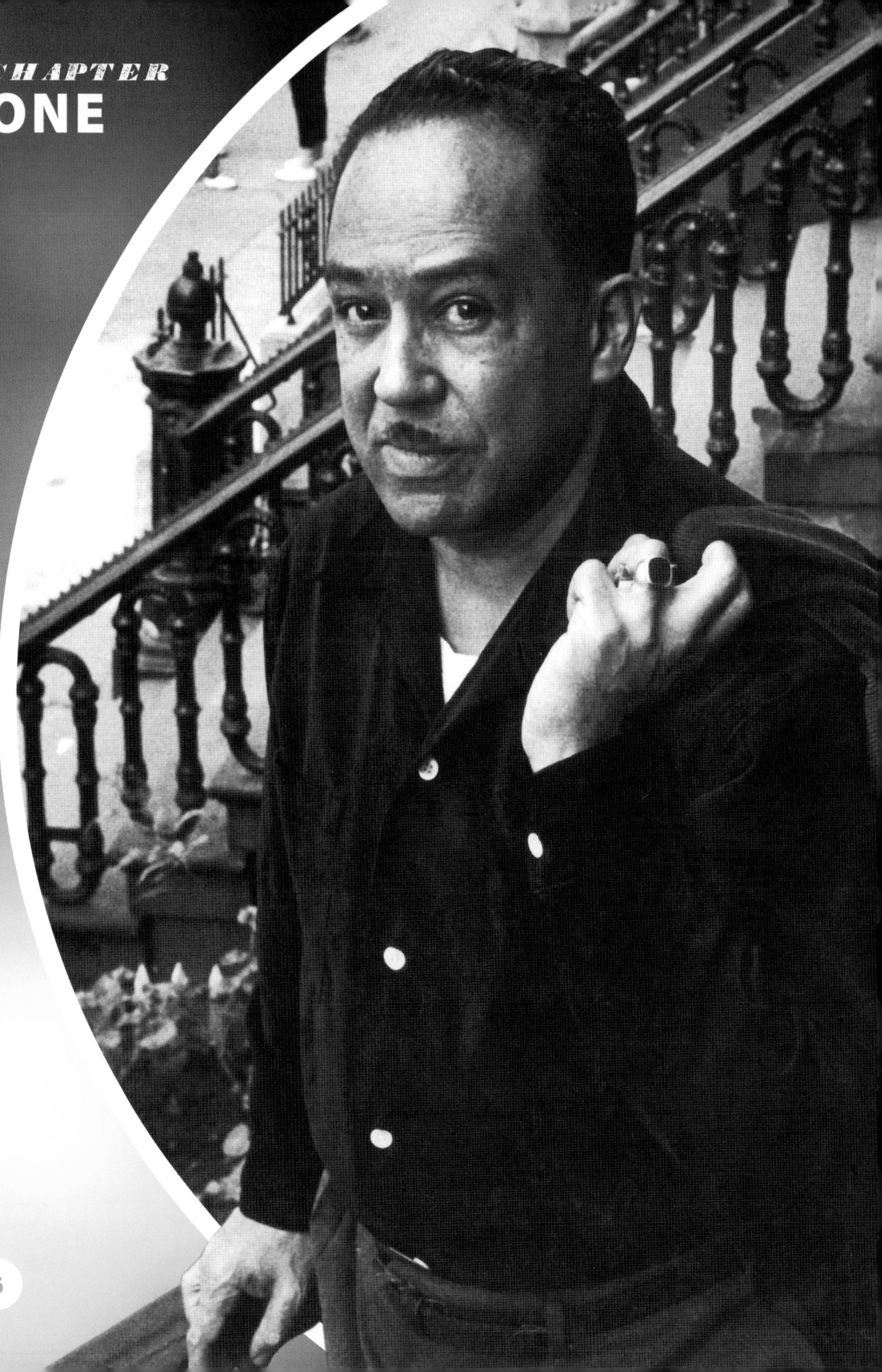

WELCOME TO PARIS

Langston Hughes first saw Paris, France, early one summer morning in 1924. Hughes had just left his job aboard a freighter ship after hearing stories about Paris from a native Frenchman. Hughes decided to visit the famous City of Lights for a few months.

Even though he only had seven dollars in his pocket, Hughes set out to see the sights. One day, he visited the Louvre. The Louvre is the world's largest art museum. Inside, Hughes saw statues from ancient Greece. In his autobiography, Hughes said that he talked to one statue. He told it, "If you can stay in Paris as long as you've been here and look OK,

Writer Langston Hughes lived in New York City before he left to travel abroad in 1923.

I guess I can stay a while with seven dollars and make a go of it."

A LONG HISTORY

African Americans had visited France long before Hughes made his trip. In the 1800s, a community of free and wealthy Creoles lived in Louisiana. Louisiana Creoles were the descendants of French or Spanish nobles and black or Native American women. Most US schools wouldn't accept Creoles because of the color of their skin. Creoles had to find other options for schooling. Many Creoles sent their children to France for their educations. They were accepted into French society.

Throughout the late 1800s and early 1900s, important members of the African American community also went to France. African American leaders Frederick Douglass, Booker T. Washington, and W. E. B. Du Bois all visited the country. When they came home, they told everyone about how well they were treated.

Activist Frederick Douglass traveled to France to give speeches in the late 1800s.

Their experiences inspired other African Americans to visit France.

WHY FRANCE?

The saying "There are no slaves in France" has been popular in the country since the 1500s. This saying is not completely true. African people were enslaved in French colonies until the mid-1800s. But this saying shows

James Weldon Johnson was an African American poet, novelist, and songwriter. He wrote the song "Lift Every Voice and Sing" in 1900. This song became popular in the black community. It was later named the Black National Anthem. It helped motivate activists during the American civil rights movement. In Johnson's autobiography, he recalled how he felt the first time he visited France in 1905. He wrote, "I became aware of the working of a miracle within me. . . . I recaptured for the first time since childhood the sense of being just a human being."

how deeply ideas of equality and freedom are rooted in French culture. Equality is even in the French national motto: *liberté, égalité, fraternité*. This means "liberty, equality, brotherhood."

In contrast, the United States has a long history of slavery and racism. Enslaved African Americans were not freed until 1865. The Thirteenth Amendment, which ended slavery, was passed that year. Then in the late 1870s, states passed Jim Crow laws to keep African Americans from using their rights. These laws segregated black people in public places, such as restaurants. Black people didn't have access to the same goods and services as white people. Black people in the United States continued to be mistreated throughout the 1900s. This mistreatment would become even clearer when black soldiers arrived in France during World War I (1914–1918).

LIBERTÉ, ÉGALITÉ, FRATERNITÉ

In the 1700s, peasants made up the biggest and poorest group in French society. They had to give most of the money they earned to wealthy people. In 1789 a group of peasants stormed a prison in Paris. This prison was called the Bastille. The peasants demanded that the French king give them more rights. One of the slogans the peasants used was *liberté, égalité, fraternité*. It symbolized their dream of freedom from poverty and equality for all. The storming of the Bastille led to the French Revolution (1789–1799). As a result of this revolution, French citizens achieved greater freedoms.

CHAPTER TWO

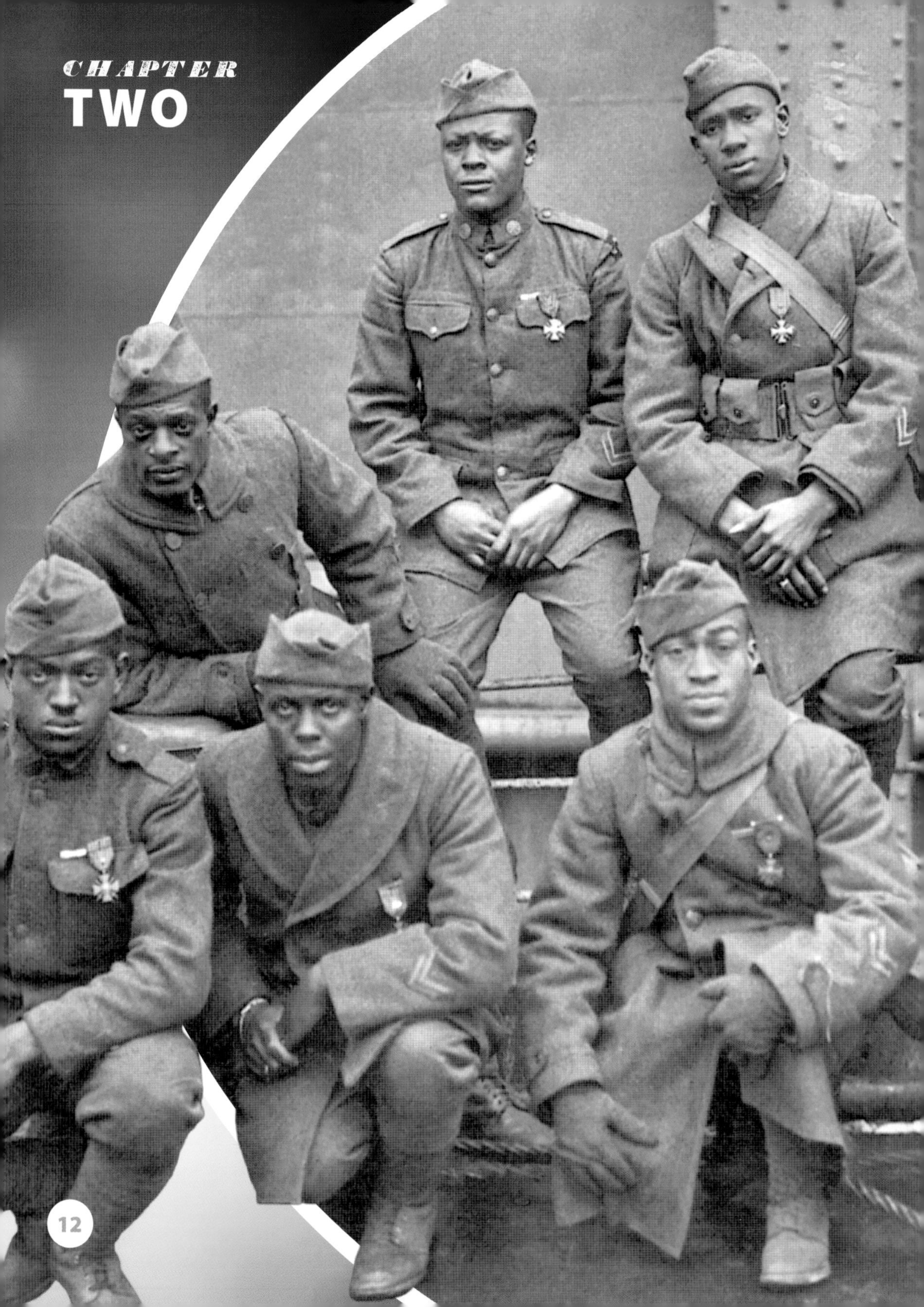

THE SOLDIERS

Until 1948 the US military was segregated. White and black soldiers weren't allowed to fight, sleep, or eat together. Still, hundreds of thousands of African Americans volunteered to serve their country during World War I. More than 200,000 African Americans served in France during the war. African Americans hoped that serving their country would bring black people recognition. They thought this might result in the US government granting black people their rights.

African American soldiers fought in separate combat groups in World War I.

SERVICE IN WORLD WAR I

Many African American soldiers wanted to fight in World War I. But US military leaders didn't think black soldiers were as capable as white soldiers. President Woodrow Wilson believed that black people shouldn't hold positions of authority in the army. Most black soldiers were forced to do noncombat tasks. They dug ditches and buried dead bodies. This was important but hard work. Discrimination from white troops made it even harder.

The 369th Infantry Regiment's jazz band performs in France in 1918.

Approximately 40,000 black soldiers in the US Army did fight in World War I. They belonged to the Ninety-Second and the Ninety-Third divisions. These were two black combat groups. The Ninety-Third's 369th Infantry Regiment from New York became the most famous black fighting unit. They were nicknamed the "Harlem Hellfighters." The name came from a black neighborhood called Harlem in New York City.

WORLD WAR II

German ruler Adolf Hitler invaded Poland in 1939. This invasion triggered World War II (1939–1945). The United States joined the war in 1941. African Americans once again went abroad to fight for their country. More than 1 million African Americans served in World War II. Some of them fought in France. Many African Americans who lived in France fled the country. Hitler disliked jazz music because it had come from the United States. The United States was one of Germany's enemies. Hitler's Nazi Party banned jazz music. Many jazz musicians fled France because they feared imprisonment.

The regiment was known for its tough fighters. France later gave the regiment the Croix de Guerre award. This is the country's highest military honor. The regiment's jazz band performed for British, French, and US troops in France. Jazz music helped raise soldiers' spirits during the war.

THE RED SUMMER

When African American soldiers came home, they found that their service didn't protect them from prejudice. Racism was still everywhere. White mobs killed approximately 50 black people from January to

September 1919. Race riots broke out in the summer and fall of 1919. These fights were caused by a hatred of one race toward another. White people attacked black people during these riots in cities throughout the country. The summer and fall of 1919 were marked by widespread violence in the United States. This period became known as the "Red Summer."

Black veterans defended black communities during the Red Summer. They stood up against mob violence. Approximately 100,000 black veterans moved from the South to the North. They hoped to encounter less violence in the North. But they were still segregated and discriminated against there. Their sacrifices abroad had not resulted in better treatment at home.

In the face of such prejudice, black soldiers remembered France fondly. They wrote articles about France in American newspapers. Some of them returned to live in France after the war. Some attended universities in France. Other soldiers who were also

BLACK MILITARY SERVICE

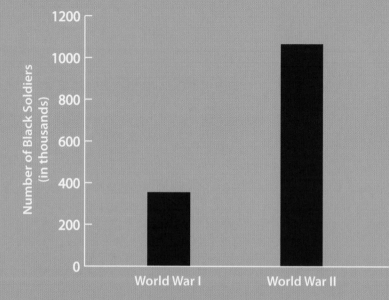

African Americans played important roles in both World War I and World War II. The chart above shows the number of African Americans who served in these wars. African Americans faced violence and discrimination at home. Yet they still continued to serve their country in large numbers. Why do you think this was?

musicians returned to France to play music. In Europe these ex-soldiers were often paid well to play music. They helped make jazz music popular in France, and some even landed record deals. This paved the way for the black artists who came to Paris in the 1920s and 1930s.

STRAIGHT TO THE
SOURCE

William Colson was a black officer who fought in France during World War I. In a newspaper article, he described what he called the "negro" soldier's experience in France. Although the term *negro* is widely seen as offensive today, it was commonly used in the early 1900s. Colson wrote:

> The French took the negro soldiers on terms of absolute equality. . . . The French people opened their homes welcomely to them. They wined and dined them at every opportunity. . . . Remembering the pleasantness of French life, [the African American] will not rest until he has caused to be ushered into the United States a state of complete and uncompromising economic, political, and social equality.

Source: Lieut. William N. Colson. "The Social Experience of the Negro Soldier Abroad." *The Messenger*. HathiTrust Digital Library, October 1919. Web. Accessed July 12, 2018. 27.

What's the Big Idea?
Read the text carefully. What is the main idea? What points did Colson use to support this idea? How do you think Colson viewed his military service in France?

CHAPTER
THREE

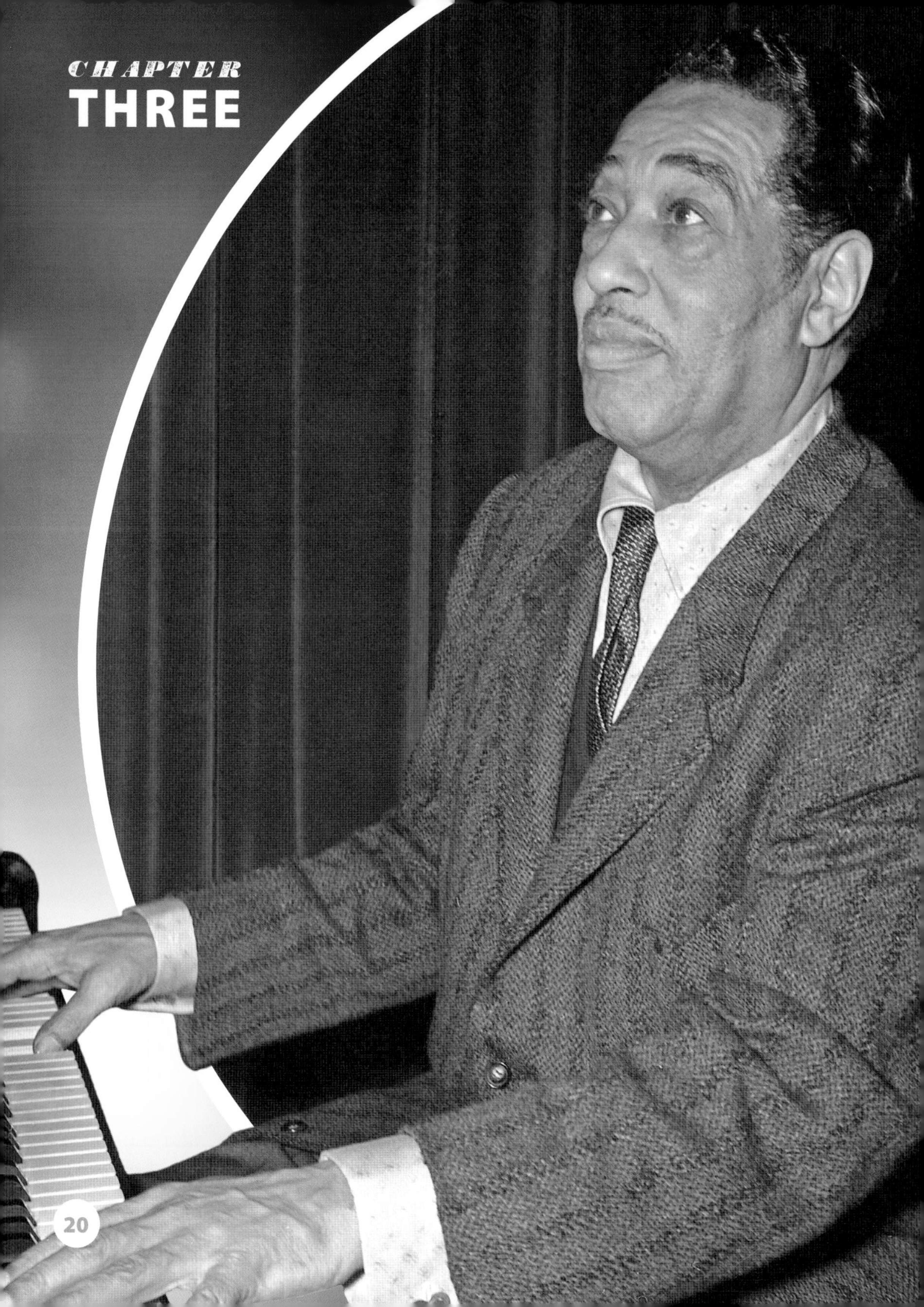

THE PERFORMERS

Many black performers came to Paris during the 1920s and 1930s. This period was known as the Jazz Age. African American jazz performers wowed audiences with their music and styles.

As Paris's black community grew, many African Americans took notice and moved there. Some of the best-known African Americans who settled in Paris were dancers and musicians. Many were drawn to the city's nightclub scene and launched their careers performing in famous nightclubs.

African American jazz musicians such as piano player Duke Ellington often performed in Paris.

JAZZ

Jazz is an American style of music. It started in black communities in the South in the early 1900s. Jazz combines different kinds of music, including blues and ragtime. Jazz often involves improvisation, or making things up. A band plays a melody while one musician makes up his part on the spot. Jazz can express many different feelings, from sadness to joy.

QUEEN OF THE NIGHTCLUBS

One of the most famous members of the Paris jazz scene was Ada "Bricktop" Smith. Smith was born in West Virginia in 1894. She left home at the age of 16 to become a dancer and jazz singer. She toured across the country. Then she moved to New York City. A nightclub owner there nicknamed her "Bricktop" because of her red hair.

In 1924 Smith performed at a small Paris nightclub called Le Grand Duc. Eugene Bullard managed the club. He was a drummer and the first African American fighter pilot. He began working at the club after flying planes for France in World War I.

Ada "Bricktop" Smith stands outside one of her nightclubs in Paris in the 1930s.

Smith helped make Le Grand Duc famous. Black jazz musicians such as trumpet player Louis Armstrong also performed at the club. Smith gave dance lessons to celebrities who visited the club. One of her students was the future King Edward VIII of England.

Smith saved the money she earned from teaching dance lessons. Her friend Cole Porter, an American composer, also lent her money. Smith used these funds to open her first nightclub in Paris in 1926. She named it Chez Bricktop.

Chez Bricktop was a magnet for celebrities and Paris's black community. Black entertainers played there to packed crowds. These entertainers included piano player Duke Ellington and singer Josephine Baker. Chez Bricktop did so well that Smith opened more nightclubs around Paris.

After Hitler invaded Poland in 1939, starting World War II (1939–1945), Smith sold her clubs. She moved back to New York City. She tried to start over there. But it was much harder to be a black nightclub owner in the United States than in Paris. Smith opened nightclubs around the world until her death in 1984. But none were ever as successful as Chez Bricktop.

JOSEPHINE BAKER

Josephine Baker was another well-known black entertainer who settled in Paris in the 1920s. She grew up in Saint Louis, Missouri, in the early 1900s. Her birth name was Freda Josephine McDonald. Her family was poor. Freda left school when she was eight to start working. She babysat and cleaned houses for rich white people. The work was hard. Her employers often treated Freda badly.

In 1919 Freda left Saint Louis for New York. She wanted to escape racial violence in the South. She supported herself by working as a chorus girl and a waitress. In 1921 she married a man named Willie Baker. When that marriage ended, Freda kept his last name. She also stopped using her first name and instead went by Josephine Baker.

Baker sang and danced in vaudeville musicals and comedy sketches. She performed throughout the

Josephine Baker performs on stage with an elephant at a Paris theater in 1968.

United States. In 1925 she traveled to Paris to perform in a show.

Baker couldn't have picked a better time to be in Paris. When black soldiers introduced jazz to France during World War I, they set off a nationwide obsession. Black culture fascinated the French. They were

especially interested in African American music and dance. Their interest was so intense it was given a name. It was called *le tumulte noir*, or "the black craze."

Le tumulte noir created many job opportunities for black artists in Paris. But it had negative aspects too. The craze was based on stereotypes of

African Americans. The French sometimes compared African Americans to animals. They called African Americans "wild" and "untamed." The French thought that these qualities made African Americans great singers and performers.

Baker knew what Parisian audiences expected of her. She used their stereotypes to her advantage. She sometimes danced wildly in her shows. She waved her arms, crossed her eyes, or stuck out her tongue. In her most famous dance routine, she dressed in a skirt made out of bananas.

Baker was a hit in Paris. Her fans gave her nicknames such as "Black Pearl" and "Black Venus." She began touring around Europe. Baker soon became the highest-paid chorus girl in vaudeville.

Baker later married a Frenchman. She became a French citizen. She was a spy for the French Resistance during World War II. The French Resistance fought against the Nazi German occupation. Baker carried secret messages for the resistance. She hid them in her sheet music.

Baker returned to the United States in the 1950s. The racism she saw there shocked her. She refused to perform for segregated audiences. She supported the American civil rights movement. In 1963 she spoke at the March on Washington in Washington, DC. This was a protest march and rally for black civil rights. Baker later returned to Paris. She died there in 1975. Thousands of people attended her funeral.

EXPLORE ONLINE

Chapter Three discusses Josephine Baker and her popularity in France. The article below also goes into more depth on this topic. As you know, every source is different. What information does the website give about Josephine Baker? How is the information from the website the same as the information in Chapter Three? What new information did you learn from the website?

ABOUT JOSEPHINE BAKER
abdocorelibrary.com/blacks-in-paris

CHAPTER
FOUR

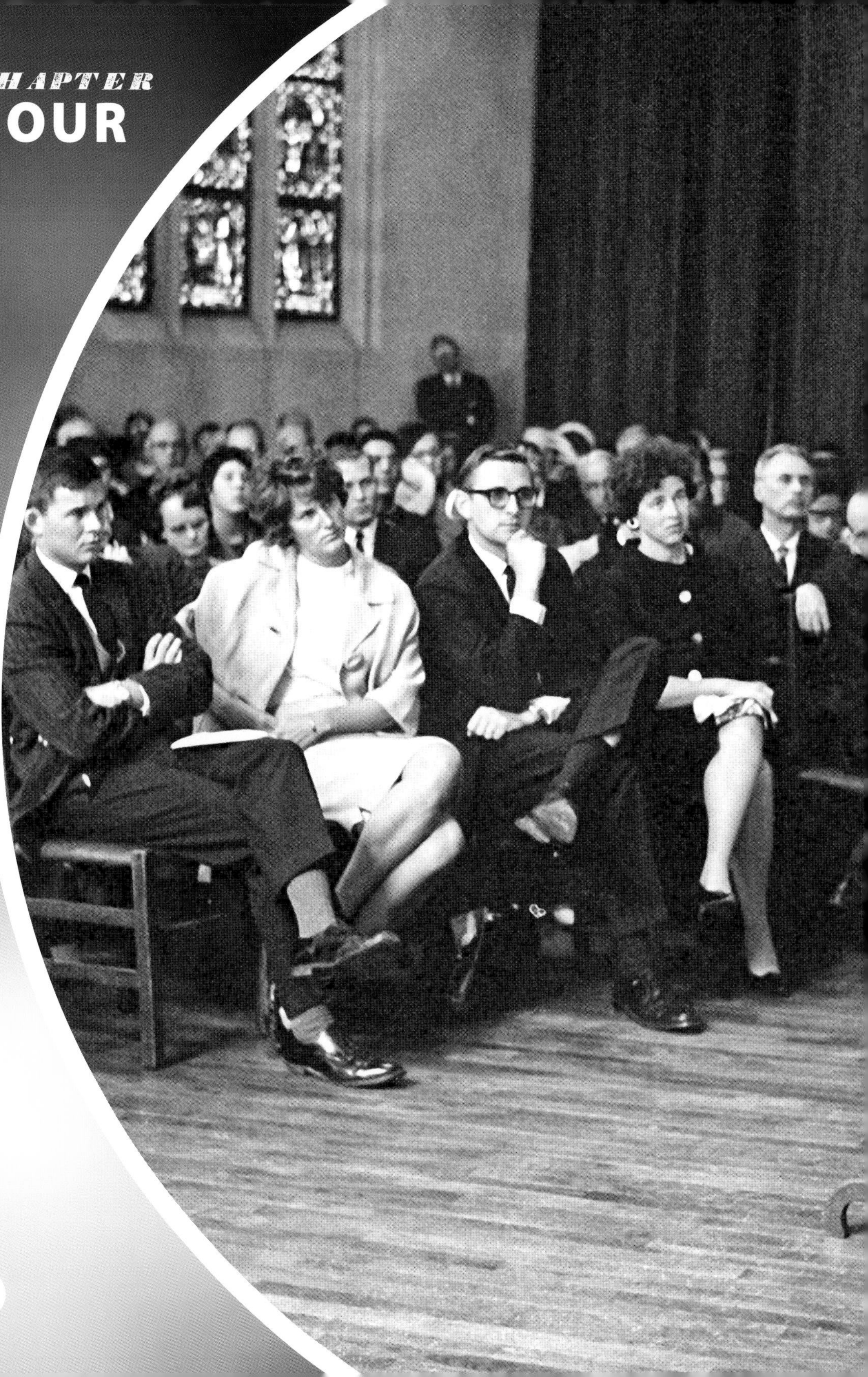

THE WRITERS

Many African American writers have lived in or visited Paris. Most of these writers came in one of two waves. The first wave was during the Jazz Age. The second wave of writers came in the years after World War II.

THE JAZZ AGE WRITERS

Langston Hughes and many other African American writers spent time in Paris in the 1920s. Writers had heard stories about France from World War I veterans, jazz musicians, and others in the black community. Black writers were attracted to the promise of freedom and equality. Few of them

Writer James Baldwin gives a speech at a church in Paris in 1963.

stayed in Paris for very long. Some left due to a lack of funds. Others left to explore other countries.

Many black writers stayed in Paris's Montmartre district. This area was so popular with African Americans that it was known as the "Harlem of the City of Lights." The freedom and excitement black writers found in Paris inspired them. They also enjoyed the friendly welcome they received from Parisians.

POSTWAR PARIS

Many well-known black writers came to Paris after World War II. Among the

PERSPECTIVES

"HOME" FEELING

Gwendolyn Bennett was a black writer and artist who lived in Paris in the 1920s. She loved the city but was sometimes homesick. In her journal, she explained her mixed feelings about the United States. "There are times I'd give half my remaining years to hear the 'Star-Spangled Banner,'" she wrote. "And yet when I feel that way, I know it has nothing to do with the same 'home' feeling I have when I see crowds of American white people."

Author Richard Wright used Paris as a setting in some of his novels.

most famous of these writers were Richard Wright and James Baldwin. Wright was born in Mississippi in 1908. His grandparents had been enslaved during the American Civil War (1861–1865). His family was poor. Wright used his writing to protest the mistreatment of black people.

Wright moved to Paris in 1946. He became friends with other black writers in Paris, including Baldwin. Baldwin had moved from New York City to Paris in 1948. He left the United States to escape discrimination and focus on his writing. By the time he arrived in France, he had already written many plays, stories, and essays. But Baldwin didn't have much money. He didn't know the French language.

Wright met Baldwin on Baldwin's first day in Paris. The two writers met at a café called Les Deux Magots. Wright introduced Baldwin to the editors of a literary magazine. They were interested in publishing Baldwin's work. They supported Baldwin as he adjusted to life in a new city.

Wright never returned to the United States. Baldwin went back many times, especially in the 1950s and 1960s. He supported the civil rights movement. But unlike most black writers in Paris, neither Wright nor Baldwin ever permanently lived in the United States again.

BALDWIN AND WRIGHT

Baldwin and Wright didn't always agree. Baldwin once published an essay that criticized Wright's novel *Native Son*. Baldwin later ran into Wright in a café. Wright was angry with Baldwin. He said Baldwin had betrayed him and the black community. But the two men eventually made up and remained lifelong friends.

STRAIGHT TO THE
SOURCE

James Baldwin observed that the black community in Paris wasn't very close. In his essay "Encounter on the Seine," he argued that this lack of closeness meant that African Americans in Paris were isolated. He said:

> In general, only the [black] entertainers are able to maintain a useful and unquestioning comradeship with other [black people]. Their nonperforming, [black] countrymen are, nearly to a man, incomparably more isolated, and it must be conceded that this isolation is deliberate. . . . It is altogether inevitable that past humiliations should become associated not only with one's traditional oppressors but also with one's traditional kinfolk. Thus the sight of a face from home is not invariably a source of joy, but can also quite easily become a source of embarrassment or rage.

Source: James Baldwin. "Encounters on the Seine: Black Meets Brown." *Notes of a Native Son*. Boston: Beacon Press, 1984. Print. 118.

Back It Up

Baldwin used evidence in his essay to support a point. Write a paragraph describing the point Baldwin was making. Then write down two or three pieces of evidence he used to make the point.

BLACKS IN PARIS TODAY

Many African Americans today remain fascinated by Paris. Black musicians mention the city in songs. Black celebrities such as tennis star Serena Williams have homes there. Most African Americans still face less discrimination in France than in the United States. But many people of African descent who live in France today experience racism.

AFRICANS IN FRANCE

Like many European countries, France once had colonies in Africa. French is the official first or second language in 26 African countries.

A tour guide talks to a group of black tourists about the history of African Americans in Paris.

Many Africans who move to France do not encounter a language barrier. But they do experience widespread racism. People with African- or foreign-sounding last names are regularly turned down for jobs. Afro-French children are often discouraged from attending top schools.

Even black government officials in France can experience racism. Christiane Taubira was the Justice Minister of France for four years. She was born in French Guiana, a territory of France in South America. She is a French citizen by birth. In 2013 a political candidate made racist comments about Taubira. A French magazine compared her to a monkey. People even waved bananas at her at a political rally. These events show how black people continue to face discrimination in many countries, including France.

A LASTING LEGACY

Despite these problems, many African Americans visit and move to Paris today. They can trace the history of influential African Americans who came before them. Visitors can go on walking tours of Montmartre. They can swim in a pool

CELEBRATING BLACK CULTURE

Negritude is a cultural and literary movement. It is based on the belief that blackness and African culture are valuable and important. Aimé Césaire, Léopold Sédar Senghor, and Léon-Gontran Damas founded the negritude movement in the 1930s. All three were black graduate students from French colonies. They met in 1931 while studying in Paris. They were influenced by black writers, including Langston Hughes and Richard Wright.

BLACK CULTURE IN PARIS

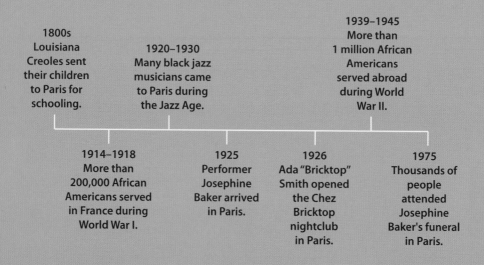

1800s
Louisiana Creoles sent their children to Paris for schooling.

1920–1930
Many black jazz musicians came to Paris during the Jazz Age.

1939–1945
More than 1 million African Americans served abroad during World War II.

1914–1918
More than 200,000 African Americans served in France during World War I.

1925
Performer Josephine Baker arrived in Paris.

1926
Ada "Bricktop" Smith opened the Chez Bricktop nightclub in Paris.

1975
Thousands of people attended Josephine Baker's funeral in Paris.

The above timeline explores important events and people that influenced black culture in Paris. How did these events and people shape Parisian society? How can their influence be seen in Paris today?

named after Josephine Baker. They can explore places that were important to black artists, such as Café de Flore. James Baldwin wrote his novel *Go Tell It on the Mountain* in this famous coffee shop.

African Americans can also explore the influence of these figures in the United States. Sidney Bechet's music has appeared in many movies, including the award-winning French film *Amélie*. Best-selling African

American author Ta-Nehisi Coates says Baldwin influenced his writing. Black singers such as Diana Ross and Rihanna have taken fashion inspiration from Josephine Baker. Pop star Beyoncé even performed in a banana skirt on national television. In these ways, the voices of the many African Americans who have called Paris home still echo today.

FURTHER EVIDENCE

Chapter Five covers the cultural influence of African Americans who lived in Paris. What was one of the chapter's main points? What evidence supports this point? Read the article at the website below. Does the information on the website support this point? Or does it present new evidence?

AFRICAN AMERICANS IN PARIS
abdocorelibrary.com/blacks-in-paris

FAST FACTS

- African Americans have been living in Paris for hundreds of years.

- The idea of equality has been part of French culture since the 1500s.

- African American soldiers who fought in World War I introduced jazz music to France.

- Thousands of African Americans served abroad in France during World War I and World War II.

- African Americans faced discrimination and violence in the United States throughout the 1900s. Many came to Paris to escape that racism and have greater freedoms.

- Many black entertainers, such as Josephine Baker, came to Paris during the Jazz Age in the 1920s and 1930s.

- Many black writers traveled to Paris during the Jazz Age. Others, such as James Baldwin, settled in Paris after World War II. Their experiences in Paris inspired their writings.

- French people of African descent still face racism in France today.

STOP AND
THINK

Tell the Tale

Chapter Three covers black performers who came to Paris during the Jazz Age. Imagine you are attending a jazz performance in Paris in the 1920s. Write 200 words about your experience. Who would you meet?

Surprise Me

Chapter Two discusses the experiences of African American soldiers fighting abroad during World War I and World War II. After reading this chapter, what two or three facts about this topic did you find most surprising? Write a few sentences about each fact. Why did you find them surprising?

Dig Deeper

After reading this book, what questions do you still have about African Americans in Paris? With an adult's help, find a few reliable sources that can help you answer your questions. Write a paragraph about what you learned.

GLOSSARY

anthem
a song of praise and pride

colony
a place that belongs to a faraway nation

discrimination
the unjust treatment of a person or group based on race or other perceived differences

occupation
the takeover and control of an area

prejudice
a dislike for a group of people due to a certain characteristic, such as their race

racism
a belief that certain people are better than others because of their race or ethnicity

segregated
separated from others, often because of race, religion, or gender

stereotypes
common beliefs about a group of people that are usually negative and untrue

vaudeville
a kind of stage performance that includes songs, dances, and comedy acts

ONLINE RESOURCES

To learn more about African Americans in Paris, visit our free resource websites below.

Visit **abdocorelibrary.com** for free Common Core resources for teachers and students, including vetted activities, multimedia, and booklinks, for deeper subject comprehension.

Visit **abdobooklinks.com** for free additional online weblinks for further learning. These links are routinely monitored and updated to provide the most current information available.

LEARN MORE

Anderson, Jennifer Joline. *Langston Hughes*. Minneapolis, MN: Abdo Publishing, 2013.

Powell, Patricia Hruby. *Josephine: The Dazzling Life of Josephine Baker*. San Francisco: Chronicle Books, 2014.

ABOUT THE
AUTHORS

Duchess Harris, JD, PhD

Professor Harris is the chair of the American Studies department at Macalester College and curator of the Duchess Harris Collection of ABDO books. She is the author and coauthor of recently released ABDO books including *Hidden Human Computers: The Black Women of NASA*, *Black Lives Matter*, and *Race and Policing*.

Before working with ABDO, she authored several other books on the topics of race, culture, and American history. She served as an associate editor for *Litigation News*, the American Bar Association Section of Litigation's quarterly flagship publication, and was the first editor in chief of *Law Raza*, an interactive online journal covering race and the law, published at William Mitchell College of Law. She has earned a PhD in American Studies from the University of Minnesota and a JD from William Mitchell College of Law.

Anitra Budd

Anitra Budd is a writer, editor, and educator. She has written books and articles for young people and adults. She enjoys reading, sewing, and learning new languages.

INDEX